An Invitation
To
The Wilderness

An Invitation
To
The Wilderness

Is There A Dream?

Marisa D. Matthews

AN INVITATION TO THE WILDERNESS

For more information or to contact the author write to:
Deeper Life Ministries International, Inc.
P.O. Box 526370
Dept 21-0186
Miami, FL 33152
Email : info@deeperlifeministriesintl.org

Book and Cover design by M. D. Matthews
Front and back cover Judean Desert photo © Canstock.com

ISBN-13: 978-0692489925
ISBN-10 : 0692489924

First Edition: July 2015

CONTENTS

DEDICATION

To two of the most influential people in my life, Annie Bell Matthews (Grandma Anne), and the late Arleva M. Rainey (Big Mama). I will forever cherish our lunch meetings where your godly wisdom and counsel helped me become solidified in my faith in God. Your loving support encouraged me to keep moving forward no matter what comes my way. I thank you for that gift of **perseverance**.

FORWARD

In every generation, God will raise up a voice to speak His plan and His thoughts for that particular era. We see Moses during the time of the Hebrew captivity in Egypt demanding Pharaoh as instructed by God the Father to "let His people go." We see John the Baptist in the New Testament era speaking in the Judean wilderness to a wicked and idolatrous generation in Matt. 2:2-3 to *"repent and prepare ye the way of the Lord."*

In our 21st century society of unbridled lust, materialism, and hedonism, there is a cry, a clarion call released from the Spirit of the living God through Minister Marisa D. Matthews to come away into the wilderness. What is the wilderness? Merriam-Webster's dictionary states *"an uncultivated and uninhabited region; a wild or desolate place."* When we look at our lives today as Believers, we recognize that there are many uncultivated, wild, and desolate places in us.

This book that you are preparing to embark on will allow you to meet the Spirit of the living God in such a way that purpose will be rediscovered, dreams that were lost can be renewed, and life as promised by Jesus in John 10:10 will be full: *"The thief cometh not, but for to steal, and to kill, and to destroy: I*

am come that they might have life, and that

they might have it more abundantly."

So come along, I invite you to enter the

wilderness.

Claudette M. Basden, Senior Pastor
A Touch of Love Ministries International Center, Inc.
Providenciales, Turks and Caicos Islands, BWI
July 14, 2015

INTRODUCTION

"In the wilderness lies preparation."

When I think of the word "wilderness" my immediate thought creates a vision of a dark forest, damp grounds, and echoes of an owl perched and preening on a limb above. In the dark of night, an individual all alone slowly ebbs their way through the path. I know too many Alfred Hitchcock thrillers. Other images that come to mind depict a long stretch of deserted, parched land. In the distance, you can see an individual slowly dragging their way through a path that appears to have no

end. The sun is beating incessantly upon their head

and cooking the insects on the ground at the same

time. Delirium begins to creep into their mind as

they make their way.

Believe it or not your wilderness experience may

at times resemble just what I have described above.

However, even in the dreariness of the moment,

there lies a twinkle of moonlight cresting over the

mountain high above and breaking through the

expanse of trees and glistening on the earth's floor.

It is in this light that you realize that your current

experience is but for a moment. How long is a

moment? Well, that depends on you. However,

upon successful completion of your journey through

the wilderness you can emerge brighter, better,

stronger, smarter, liberated **or** you can become

bewildered, disenchanted, and discouraged. Although, these feelings are contingent upon your acceptance or rejection of the new and unknown horizons that await.

The purpose of the wilderness experience(s) (yes, plural because there will be many) in your life are to prepare you for what lies ahead. Jeremiah 29:11 reminds us that God has a predetermined plan for each of our lives. The plan does not just happen, believe it or not; you have a say in the matter. More importantly only you can show up for your future. Your outcome is your acceptance or rejection of God's instructions as presented to you via the everyday choices that you make.

Truthfully, I had no intentions of writing this book; it was the furthest thing from my mind. But when I got up on January 1, 2015, and was going through some old teaching notes, I was impressed to start writing. In the course of the ensuing months, this book began to take shape.

I would like to invite you to come along on this journey as I endeavor to expound upon some biblical wilderness experiences that may be familiar to you. I also hope to share a few nuggets from my personal experiences over the years. You will find the words *wilderness* and *process* used interchangeably throughout the book. No, I was not confused. Dependent upon the subject matter each word seemed to provide a clearer representation of what I was trying to convey at the time. My prayer is that you will come away encouraged to know that:

1. You are not the only one on *Wilderness Drive.*

2. Dawn always breaks after midnight.

3. There is a deeper lesson in **every** lesson.

4. The length of the journey is dependent upon your choice of embracing or rejecting the process.

5. Outward compliance has no effect on inward commitment. It's a *heart* thing.

6. There is always someone that can learn from what you have gone through. Thus, your experiences **have value.**

Welcome, I invite you to the wilderness, your journey awaits…

CHAPTER ONE

Where It All Began

N o one could have imagined that the little girl born to William and Dorothy Matthews at Letterman's Army Hospital in San Francisco, California in April of 1960, would someday grow up to challenge the *status quo*. Merriam- Webster's dictionary defines the *status quo* as *"the current situation; the way things are now"* or as I surmise, those things presently perpetrating as "life". Here it is January 2015 approaching the advent of my 55th birthday, and I am more eager and ready to challenge life!

Now, before I get ahead of myself, allow me to rewind and let you know that "status quo" at one time in my journey was my fixed destination. What had always been drummed into my head as a child was: *"get an education and get a good job with benefits."* And, if you so choose, have a family and retire comfortably. While that all sounds pretty sensible, and it works quite well for some, I am convinced it was not the path intended for me. I must say, and I am sure my parents would agree, that most of my life I have been one to challenge the *status quo* or what others may deem to be the *norm. Norm,* according to Merriam-Webster's dictionary is *"something that is usual, typical, or* *standard; an <u>average</u> level of development or achievement; a way of doing something that is <u>usual</u> or <u>expected</u>.*" The "norm" in this instance for me is not very appealing. Average is not something I aspire to be neither does it invoke fulfillment or adventure for me. As I continued to follow my dream, I realized that the norm was an enemy of my destiny and a robber of my future. At age 30, I began my quest. I realized that life was about passion, about purpose, and about making a difference in your sphere of influence while you are here on earth. It is so easy to settle into the daily grind and tell yourself that "I'll get to it later, or I'll do that one day." Only to find the one day has come and gone and time is no longer your friend.

My mantra has always been that at the sunset of my life I never want to speak the words "I wish I would have…" The choices you make daily, and your willingness to commit and do something of purpose or your lack of commitment forms the legacy of your life.

It is not how long you live but the quality and manner in which you live between the dates. When you visit a graveyard, the first thing you notice is the date of birth, and the date of death etched on the tombstone. Looking at that period of time you surmise how long the individual lived. But when you think about it, it does not matter whether you lived a hundred years or twenty, the real sense of purpose lies in **how** you lived between the dates.

What will your legacy be? How will you be remembered by friends, family, loved ones, community, business colleagues, etc.? As much as you may feel your life is yours, it is not. You have to acknowledge that what you do and who you are affects others in your sphere of influence. What will history write about you?

"There is no passion to be found playing small – in settling for life that is less than the one you are capable of living."

Nelson Mandela

Today, while settling into my new home and clearing out some old files, I found a message I shared at a conference in the Turks and Caicos Islands (TCI) on December 8, 2007. Wow! That was over seven years ago and only five months after I relocated to TCI from Chicago, Illinois. The question I asked during the conference was: *"How many of you have a dream?"* And uncanny as it may seem that question still resonates today. I believe everyone has a dream, and everyone has a purpose. God so plainly tells us in Jer. 29:11, *"I know the plans I have for you; plans to prosper you and not to harm you, plans of hope and a future and an expected end."* (Amplified Bible)

"The only time it is too late to make a change is when you are dead."

Marisa D. Matthews

However, when people glimpse or sense that the path to that dream may hold difficulties or hardships many will chose what I call the *path of least resistance.* In essence, it is any path but the one that will cause you to exert yourself, make a commitment, or require you to give up something or someone. It is a path that is comfortable, we all know it well and it doesn't require anything from us.

Now, after years of traveling down the path of least resistance, you find yourself in unpleasant situations. They include jobs, relationships, and a host of other negative things; far removed from the dream that long ago burned so deeply inside you. As depressing as it may seem, there is still time to get back on track, get focused, and get moving again. The only time it is too late to make a change is when you are dead; that my friend is the true reality.

So I ask again, *"How many of you have a dream?"* Do you honestly believe, stand confident and are assured that currently in your life you have everything you need to bring that dream into a reality for your life? I would venture to say the answer is no. I remember a slogan I read on a ball cap when I was visiting a mall in Dallas, Texas many years ago, and it read *"Life is a journey, not a guided tour."* That message has stayed with me over the years and has helped me to remain engaged in my life's plan. So many people today want to stay on the tour bus of life (i.e. content with sightseeing and living life on the surface never engaging life itself), and still expect to fulfill their purpose and destiny. Honk! Honk! It is not going to happen. There are so many little things that get you side-tracked from your purposeful path in life. Paul said it well in Philippians when he reminded the people that purpose is found in your focus:

"Brethren, I count not myself to have apprehended: but this one thing I do, forgetting those things which are behind, and reaching forth unto those things which are before, I press toward the mark for the prize of the high calling of God in Christ Jesus." (Phil 3:13-14)

A real journey involves wilderness experiences. Believe it or not the wilderness is a good place to be because it serves as an invaluable place (season and time) of preparation. It is the place where God transforms you into the person who can *do* your dream. Always remember the larger the dream, the longer the preparation. Ouch! I know, no one wants to hear that. We are all accustomed to having things our way and done in our time. Well, answer this? How has that worked out for you thus far? Have you arrived at your destination? Is the glory of God being manifested in your life through the fruit of the Spirit? Are you an asset to the Kingdom of God? Don't answer, just think about it.

I have come to realize in my life that nothing done "in God" and "for God" can be considered the norm. I have firmly held the position for years that "God does not do normal." He is a God of the **extraordinary**. The Word plainly tells us in Isaiah 43:18-19 that God has an exit strategy for your wilderness experience: *"Remember ye not the former things, neither consider the things of old. Behold, I will do a new thing; now it shall spring forth; shall ye not know it? I will even make a way in the **wilderness**, and rivers in the desert."*

*"Wilderness experiences
embraced for what they
are, become teaching
tools and will bring forth
solutions."*

Marisa D. Matthews

Remember Joseph? He was a dreamer. In
Genesis 37:5-11, Joseph at seventeen had two
dreams that foretold his future rise in power.
However, before all the accolades of Pharaoh's
palace could be experienced he had to be prepared.
His youthful exuberance and lack of understanding
caused him to share his dream with his brothers
who envied him. Thus, he escaped death at the
hands of his brothers through the wilderness of
slavery. He was lied on by Potiphar's wife;

imprisoned, and forgotten all before his moment in time came where he was called to interpret Pharaoh's dream. Through all these experiences Joseph knew that God was with him. At age 30 he interpreted Pharaoh's dream. Now his dream he had at age seventeen was realized. Wow, thirteen years of preparation! His thirteen years of trial were well endured, as he grew and matured into his life's purpose which was to become the Prime Minister of Egypt. Not only did he interpret Pharaoh's dream, but he followed up with a suggested policy for implementation. Wilderness experiences embraced for what they are, become teaching tools and will bring forth solutions.

Many of you have to fight your way through various difficulties in your life, whether family, friends or career. You are tempted to lose heart and get frustrated when success seems to be taking longer to come than you think it should, as one hindrance after another seemingly blocks your path.

> *"If you find a path with no obstacles it probably doesn't lead anywhere."*
>
> Frank A. Clark

Contrary to popular belief, hindrances are helps in disguise. Just imagine, if one of Joseph's misfortunes or obstacles had been skipped or left out altogether, his opportunity to shine would not have come. If his brothers had not hated him; or if they did not sold him into slavery; or if he had not gone to prison, he would never have ruled in Egypt.

Not one thread in the tapestry of his life could have been left out without ruining the intricate, purposeful design of his pre-ordained destiny. In every facet of Joseph's experience, God was with him.

"You can see God from anywhere if your mind is set to love and obey Him."

A.W. Tozer

It is equally important to know that if you become comfortable with your current situation, you will never get out of it. If you focus on the situation, you will never see the solution. But, if you set your gaze on the dream, your progression out of the situation will be expedited. Keep in mind that whatever or whoever is causing your current pain,

or discomfort has no control over your future victory.
Keep your focus on your dream and do not allow
your present discomfort to cloud your vision. In
essence, as they would say in the old mobster
movies *"fa-get about it!"*

"There are plenty of difficult obstacles in your path. Don't allow yourself to become one of them."

Ralph Martson

The wilderness is a critical component to
obtaining your future state. Maturing into your life's
purpose takes time. The world is not going to sit
still and wait for you to catch up. You cannot afford
to skip one of your trials or sorrows. If you actually

think about it, in reality, there would be no summer unless there was a winter before. There must be a caterpillar before there is a butterfly. Thus, there must be a refining fire before there is pure gold.

Joseph came out of prison to reign. As a follower of Christ, you are God's servant. To reign means to serve, and the higher the place you may be called to serve, the harder the wilderness journey will be. Joseph waited thirteen long years. Those years chiseled strength of character, fortified courage and solidified conviction within his heart which enabled him to endure the following seven years of hard movement and administration throughout Egypt preparing the people for the impending famine.

You have to allow yourself, by God's help and guidance of the Holy Spirit, to go through the necessary preparation. Whether the preparation is in obscurity, in youth or whatever situation you find yourself, or for whatever call may be placed upon your life.

I believe, if the Body of Christ actually understood what a believer's life on earth should represent, it would be more open, desirous, and welcoming of opportunities for committed service. The spotlight of self-promotion would be non-existent and the desire for God's perfect will would be foremost. Whatever your destiny holds, just surrender and do it, as Joseph did his. Doing it with ardent concentration, knowing, as he did, that nothing is wasted in God. As Paul so aptly wrote in Rom. 8:28 *"all things work together for good, to them that love God, to them who are called according to His purpose."*

One thing is for sure if you choose to by-pass the preparation process because it seems to be taking too long: I encourage you to stop and recognize that the time will pass regardless. So you might as well spend it doing what is going to get you to the prize (your dream) in the end.

Let me reiterate, the larger the dream or vision, the more prepared you have to be, and only God can determine the length of time that it will take to ensure you are ready. The preparation period involves developing these characteristics as defined by Merriam-Webster's dictionary:

- **Endurance** – *the ability or strength to continue or last, especially despite fatigue, stress or other adverse conditions.*

- **Faith** – *confidence or trust in a person or thing; belief not based on proof*

- **Patience** – *the bearing of provocation, annoyance, misfortune, or pain without complaint, loss of temper, irritation, or the like; an ability or willingness to suppress restlessness or annoyance when confronted with delay*

- **Perseverance** – *steady persistence in a course of action, purpose, or state, etc., especially in spite of difficulties, obstacles, or discouragement.*

- **Resilience** – *the power or ability to return to the original form, position, etc., after being bent, compressed, or stretched. The ability to recover readily from illness, depression, adversity, or the like.*

Essentially, you have to develop the conviction that no circumstance, difficulty, or turmoil can change the truth of your dream. Nor can it change the faithfulness of God, who is the "dream giver," from guiding you to your destiny and bringing your dream to pass.

"It's always too early to quit."

Norman Vincent Peale

CHAPTER TWO

Let's Play Ball!

I would like to use sports analogies to help me envision and convey some of the processes the Lord uses to get you ready for "the dream." For instance, take U.S. Football. I will attempt to express my general overview and understanding of the game and its correlation with a Christian's spiritual walk with God. For those of you that may be reading this and are football fanatics; please do not get worked up over my oversimplification of the game. It is, after all, just an analogy.

There are fifty-two players on a team comprised of various squads such as the offense, defense, and special teams. The object of the game is to advance the ball one hundred yards into the opponent's territory and the end zone (across the goal line) for points. Before you can consider yourself worthy to be on the team you have to survive training camp (preparation time). Training camp provides the opportunity for new players and coaches to become acclimated to the new system. It also provides the younger players "newbies" an opportunity for the coaches to evaluate their skills. For the veterans, it is a chance to freshen up and get back into form. Usually, a total of seventy players are invited, comprised of:

- **Veterans** – returning members of the team or players that have years of experience with other organizations; these guys are what I like to call "time-tested." They have had a myriad of wilderness experiences and have come out victorious a higher percentage of the time.

- **Drafted rookies** – new recruits, often identified by stats, popularity and charisma are chosen by team management to come and be a part of the program they are building. These are the ones I like to call the "newbies." Often cocky, looking for an opportunity to unseat the veterans in their positions. Some have an over-inflated opinion of themselves, and they believe their press releases.

- **Free Agents** – These guys, young and old, are given a shot to try-out for the team, no guarantees. They are usually the hungriest, grateful for the opportunity and will do just about anything to make the team.

In training camp, every team member is given a playbook to memorize that is specific to the position they either play or desire to play.

In the Body of Christ, you have the same makeup of veterans, draftees, and free agents. The playbook is the Word of God which contains everything you need to transverse society. In the world, you will notice people choose the draftees (and that is true in the sense of the Church).

Men will select and venerate who they want to lead them (whether or not the individual is qualified to do so) or who will tickle their itching ear, i.e. make

them feel good. God is desirous of the free agents;
those who are hungry and will sacrifice for the sake
of the gospel. Those who are willing to go the
distance and not compromise what they believe.

I submit that the original plan of God called for
an offensive team **only** as mankind was made in
the image of God and given dominion over the land.
Gen. 1:26-28 reads:

"And God said, Let us make man in our image,
after our likeness: and let them have dominion over
the fish of the sea, and over the fowl of the air, and
over the cattle, and over all the earth, and over
every creeping thing that creepeth upon the earth."
However, because of the fall of mankind a
defensive unit and a special teams unit was added.

As training camp nears completion the
individuals who have successfully endured the

rigors of training are identified and considered for placement in the starting lineup. The game of life needs individuals that are both starters and finishers.

Now back to the mechanics of the game. Each team is given a series of possessions which consists of four downs or attempts to advance the football ten yards. The team with possession of the ball is on offense while the opposing team is on defense. It is the defense's duty to stop the offense from advancing.

In life, there are obstacles designed solely to hinder, delay, or stop outright your progression to your goal, your dream, and your destiny. The Word of God (which is the believer's playbook) is designed to help you to navigate the obstacles of life and bring balance and perspective to the

process (wilderness).

As in football where you have a head coach,

quarterback, and offensive coordinator the same

positions are available for the believers:

- The Head Coach is God the Father.

- The Quarterback, who carries the team, is

  Jesus Christ, and

- The Offensive Coordinator, who submits

  the plays to run, is the Holy Spirit.

What is so great about this team's

management is that your head coach knows the

end, He wrote the script. Your quarterback, Jesus

Christ has already tested and ran each play in the

Book thus, leaving you with a clear example and

manner in which you are to navigate the world's

field. The Holy Spirit, your offensive coordinator, is

the connector between heaven and earth. He is in the booth or on the ground with the headset waiting for the Word from heaven to then submit the right play for execution in your life. John 16:13 says:

"Howbeit when he, the Spirit of truth, is come, he will guide you into all truth: for he shall not speak of himself; but whatsoever he shall hear, that shall he speak: and he will shew you things to come."

As offensive coordinator, the Holy Spirit has a vision of the whole field and is ready, willing, and able to send the play you need at the time you need it. He is the voice speaking in your quiet hour. He is the nudge in your gut when you are not sure about a matter. He is the peace that overcomes you when you are restless in a situation. My friends, who are you listening to on your headset?

If by the end of the third down you still have quite a distance to go to cover the next ten yards you have to make a decision to either continue as you are or punt (give up the ball for a period of time). Punting in this instance is a surrendering of your will to the Holy Spirit followed by a trip to the wilderness, a time of preparation.

In essence, you may not have mastered the skills required to run the next *life* play. So rather than give the opponent an opportunity for good field position (the ability to gain a stronger foothold to wreak havoc in your life and in the situations you are currently facing) you punt the ball (surrender your will to the Holy Spirit) pushing your opponent back and causing him to start with a deficit rather than in your territory. The added distance your opponent must now travel will allow you the time to grow and mature in the things of God so when the

next opportunity arrives you will have what it takes

to move forward.

"Man must be big enough to admit his mistakes, smart enough to profit from them, and strong enough to correct them."

John Maxwell

Let us remove some angst about punting. So

often you expect things in life to go the way you

plan and when they do not you have a "freak-out"

moment. You have to stop what you are doing and

re-evaluate what is going on and consider a change

of course. Well, in a sense punting is just that. You

received the play that you were to run. There was

nothing at all wrong with the play. Remember,

Jesus Christ has already proven the success of the

script by walking it out in His life while on earth.

What happened is that you deviated from the script.

When God gives you a word by the Holy Spirit,

whether, through a friend, Pastor, acquaintance,

you are to carry out that word precisely as

communicated. Any deviation will abort its intended

purpose in your life and cause you to have to punt.

You have to be honest enough to admit your

mistakes.

The original plan called for the Body of Christ

to always be on offense, moving forward. When

you read Eph. 6:10-18 regarding the armor of the

believer, every piece provides a covering of the

front of the individual. Hence, retreating was not an intended option.

"Wherefore take unto you the whole armor of God, that ye may be able to withstand in the evil day, and having done all, to stand. Stand therefore, having your loins girt about with truth, and having on the breastplate of righteousness; And your feet shod with the preparation of the gospel of peace; Above all, taking the shield of faith, wherewith ye shall be able to quench all the fiery darts of the wicked. And take the helmet of salvation, and the sword of the Spirit, which is the word of God: Praying always with all prayer and supplication in the Spirit, and watching thereunto with all perseverance and supplication for all saints."

The challenge for you is to go against human nature which focuses on self-preservation, self-reliance, and self-will. The key word being *self*. It is *self* that will cause you to get off track and deviate from the scrip for your life. Getting off track is merely the consequence of a unyielding will, choosing your own way.

You have to change the way you think and operate when faced with unpleasant situations. Stop dreading and complaining about your wilderness experience. I challenge you to see your wilderness not as a test but as an invitation in which an express RSVP is required to:

- Grow up in understanding yourself

- Grow up in understanding God

- Grow up in your faith (for without faith it is impossible to please God)

You can respond with a "yes" and proceed on your path to destiny or respond with a "no" and look for the detour that will inevitably end with an aborted purpose. Either way it is your decision that will determine the outcome.

"If you really want to do something, you'll find a way. If you don't, you'll find an excuse."

Jim Rohn

As leaders and believers, you are to have rivers of living water springing forth life that will in turn bring life to those around you. Yet, you have become puddles drying up in the sun instead of the river of life and blessing you are called to be. Why?

Unwillingness to surrender your will to the Holy Spirit and the process that awaits.

Rivers have a current and are always moving. Even if the water appears still on the surface, the undercurrent is shifting and redefining boundaries. Although, your life to you may seem stagnate, unfulfilled, and meaningless just keep living, keep moving, because what you cannot see is more real than the things you can. Man cannot see your heart but God does and although things appear still, God is at work as the undercurrent, aligning things on your behalf. Those boundaries were once giants, impossible banks to move, but over time the water has broken down the bank and expanded its territory. And so it is with you, in Isa. 43:18-19, *"Remember ye not the former things, neither consider the things of old. Behold, I will do a **new***

thing*; now it shall spring forth; shall ye not know it? I will even make a way in the wilderness, and rivers in the desert."*

Again, the Wilderness is not a test; it is an invitation. II Chron. 16:9 states, *"For the eyes of the LORD run to and fro throughout the whole earth, to shew himself strong in the behalf of them whose heart is perfect toward him..."*

Will His eyes find you?

CHAPTER THREE

Watch Out! Giants!

Question: ***Do you fear the Giant in your life more than you trust God?***

The playbook (Bible) has everything you need to

conquer the giants in your life. It is up to you to

learn the plays and allow the Holy Spirit to help you

to execute them with precision. Interesting enough,

have you ever noticed that every wilderness test in

the Bible is followed by God saying one of the following:

- *"Then you shall know that I am the Lord your God who brings you out…" Exod. 6:7*

- *"That you may know that there is none like Me in all the earth" Exod. 9:14*

- *"That My name may be declared in all the earth" Exod. 9:16*

- *"That all the peoples of the earth may know the hand of the Lord that it is mighty" Jos. 4:24*

HELLO! God wants to be known and honored for who He is and giants are a primary opportunity to make His power and goodness known to a doubting and unbelieving world. Giants were never meant to deter you but to show forth the glory, strength, and power of God.

"Don't allow your dream to elude you or worse yet die with you. There is no time limit on the fulfillment of a dream but there is a time limit on your ability to achieve it."

Marisa D. Matthews

Remember David? David knew that of himself he was no match for Goliath, but he also knew, trusted in and relied on the Lord of hosts, the God of the armies of Israel. David had no armor, no experience, no equipment; he was not battle tested, nor was he trained (by the world's standards). One thing they both had was confidence but, the vast difference was that David's confidence was in God and not his own strength. He could face Goliath undeterred because He knew that God was with him just as He had been before when David fought the lion and the bear. If God is for you, how can you lose? (Rom. 8:31 MSG) I would like to add, who has nerve enough to be against you? The obvious answer is no one. David did not wait for Goliath to come to him; he ran straight into battle towards Goliath. David's faith in God allowed him to see Goliath from a different yet realistic perspective. Goliath was merely a mortal man defying an Almighty God. David saw the battle from God's point of view. If you look at giant problems and impossible situations from God's perspective, you realize that God will fight for you and with you. When you put things in proper perspective, you see more clearly, and you can fight more effectively.

What is amazing about the story of Goliath is, at nine feet tall and dressed in full armor he went down after one stone hit him in the forehead. Do you really think David himself, had the strength to hurl a stone upward with such velocity and precision that it would strike Goliath's forehead dead-center at his most vulnerable spot not even nicking his helmet? I tell you only God could have caused that to happen in that manner.

"Failed plans should not be interpreted as a failed vision. Visions don't change, they are only refined. Plans rarely stay the same, and are scrapped or adjusted as needed. Be stubborn about the vision, but flexible with your plan."

John Maxwell

What is the most important lesson learned here? "**With God, nothing is impossible**." The key is "getting in", "being in" and "staying in" with God. Failed plans should not be interpreted as a failed vision. Each time you retreat or choose to bypass the wilderness you are in essence saying that the giant is greater than the power of God. **NOT SO!** I dare you to pick up your stone and run towards your giant "in faith" and watch the deliverance of Almighty God on your behalf.

Do not allow your dream to elude you or worse yet die with you. There is no time limit on the fulfillment of a dream, but there is a time limit on your ability to achieve it.

CHAPTER FOUR

Get Ready, Get Ready, Get Ready!

"Your greatest challenge is not the lack of opportunity but being ready when it comes."

Author Unknown

It is not enough to get prepared; you must stay prepared. It is said that knowledge doubles every five years, so if you do not keep growing, your coping skills and abilities will not match the challenges you will face in this life. I have a news flash…preparation does not begin with what you do; it begins with what you believe. If you can see it, you can achieve it. If you believe success tomorrow begins with what you do today, you will treat today differently. A wise sailor will study the weather before he goes to sea because it is easier to avoid a storm than to get out of one.

The wilderness experience provides the environment in which you are able to hone your existing skills and gain new skills, including how to avoid unnecessary storms of life. So, when you leave the wilderness and face life's challenges, you will not be quick to flinch, tuck and run, or give up. You will have mastered what you need to stand in that pivotal moment, in the face of adversity.

The purpose of the wilderness is to "grow you up" into a mature believer. A mature believer is one who has gained the ability to anticipate problems and actively engage the help of the Holy Spirit in order to have a ready solution. Conversely, an immature believer allows the problem to meet them and tries to deal with the problem in their own strength and intellect.

Preparation is not merely an event; it is a perspective, thought life, an action. Abraham Lincoln once said:

"If I have six hours to cut down a tree I'll spend four hours sharpening my ax."

Your greatest challenge is not the lack of opportunity but being ready when it comes. Everybody wants to have what successful people have, but they are not willing to pay the price they paid to achieve it. There is a saying commonly quoted: *"You see the glory, but you don't know the story."* There is a story behind every accomplishment, every success, and every victory.

Remember Moses? Wow, what a feat! He led the children of Israel out of Egypt and across the Red Sea. How glamorous that seems and every time you see the Cecil B. DeMiles film *"The Ten Commandments"* or the Stephen Spielberg film *"The Prince of Egypt"* you are amazed at the enormity of what took place. Guess what? Moses spent eighty years in preparation for that particular job that only lasted forty years. He went from slave to the prince, from prince to pauper, then to a servant of God. He essentially had to unlearn the world's system (Egypt) and become a student of God's way. Imagine, eighty years of preparation before his divine purpose began to unfold; he was to be the deliverer of the children of Israel out of the hands of Pharaoh. Really, eighty years? Some of you cannot hold out a single day before you are troubling God with the proverbial "when" or "how long Lord?"

I guess one way to look at it is through the simple process of baking chicken. Would you want to eat chicken that just came from the fresh meat section of the grocery store, was washed, a little seasoning added and put in the oven for five minutes? Highly unlikely, right? However, when it comes to the processing of the purpose and destiny for your life you would like to superimpose upon Almighty God, the Creator and Sustainer of life, the time frame that you feel should work in your current situation. Really? Think again, the greater the work, the longer the preparation period required.

Of course it is your choice whether or not you want to be used by God for His service. I reiterate, the outcome of your life's journey is dependent upon your willingness and your complete surrender or lack thereof to follow God's plan for your life. Quoting a few scriptures and shouting "Amen" at the right time cannot and will not serve as a substitute for a surrendered will.

Believers today have fallen prey to the "me" syndrome. What is a *syndrome*? According to Merriam-Webster's dictionary a *syndrome* is: "*a set of signs that are characteristic of a condition, especially of a disease."* You are no threat to Satan neither are you effective for the Kingdom of God. When your sole focus is on material things such as "what you can get" or "what people think of you," you cannot be an effective voice for God in your realm of influence.

To be effective for God your life and your way of doing things has to decrease so the Christ way can increase in you. Paul declared to the Galatians in Gal. 2:20-21 *"I am crucified with Christ; nevertheless I live,* **yet not I, but Christ liveth in me:** *and the life which I now live in the flesh I live by the faith of the Son of God, who loved me and gave himself for me.* **I do not frustrate** *the grace of God..."* How does the believer frustrate the grace of God? By seeking his own way, by focusing on the world's things, i.e. materialism (bigger house, bigger car, and more money), acceptance, and approval.

Wait, don't shoot the messenger! These things are not wrong in and of themselves. It is the manner in which they are sought after by the believer that is wrong. The manner was already provided in Matt. 6:33 *"But **seek ye first the kingdom of God** and His righteousness, all these things shall be added unto you."* I submit, you cannot know the Kingdom of God without yielding to the Spirit of God. When you do whole-heartedly yield to the Spirit of God the desire for material things will take a back seat to your desire for abundant life in God.

Thus, if you are not or have not yielded then what material gain you have received will be lost. It is only a matter of time. Anything obtained and or achieved outside of God's will or not committed to

God is not qualified for the protection of God. God watches over His own things and He is not obligated to care for what is not His that includes people and things. Oh, that's harsh! No, that's truth. A truth that must be told to the body of Christ. There has been enough sugar coating concerning the will of God in this hour. You will note that it has been scientifically proven that too much sugar causes diabetes, and advanced diabetes can require the amputation of limbs. If you are a *part (limb)* of the body of Christ, do not allow your carnal nature to cause you to get amputated. The carnal-minded man is an enemy of God. As long as self (me, my way) reigns, death (separation from God) reigns.

The wilderness experience, when embraced, serves to provide necessary spiritual alignment for you to become less absorbed in self and the things of this world. It will cause you to develop a hunger for the things of God and the ways of God and thus making you useful for the Kingdom of God. John 15:7-8 reads: *"If ye abide in me and my words abide in you, ye shall ask what ye will and it shall be done unto you. Herein is my Father glorified, that ye **bear much fruit**; so shall ye be my disciples."* You cannot bear fruit (be useful) if you've been amputated.

When you set out to allow God to have free course in your life you will have to make some tough decisions and not everyone will understand especially those closest to you. I can distinctly recall when I received the instruction from the Lord to relocate from Chicago, Illinois to the Turks and Caicos Islands. For a long while I had been seeking directions for the next phase of my life. The word came to me while I was attending the Women of Power conference in Phoenix, AZ in February 2007. During my morning prayer I was instructed by the Holy Spirit to *"defer not to do."* All the reasons I could think of that would place a delay on my going forward in God were laid to rest when the Lord let me know *"He had them in His hand."* I then proceeded to make the necessary plans to facilitate my relocation. I had no prospect of a job in the Turks and Caicos at that time I only had the word from God to *"defer not to do."*

Many in my family did not understand and even derogatory comments were made concerning my decision to move. I did not allow the putrid remarks from those dear to me to hinder me. I learned long ago that people will curse and jeer what they do not understand. I refused to be drawn into the cesspool of ignorance. My commitment to move was not only a testament of my trust in God but also my faith in God. Remember, without faith it is impossible to please Him.

Needless to say, what God calls for He provides for. He took care of the people I was concerned about and He created a job for me in my new homeland just because I dared to listen, surrender, and obey Him.

God does not have favorites. What He has is **favor** toward those who will dare to trust Him in spite of what they see, hear, or know. God will work on the behalf of anyone willing to surrender and commit themselves to following Him as the Holy Spirit leads because the outcome is on Him.

CHAPTER FIVE

Why Is The Wilderness Necessary?

I N Deuteronomy 8:7-10, you see that the promise land was perfect. Filled with brooks of water, many fountains and springs; that flowed out of valleys and hills. A land of wheat and barley, of vines, fig trees, and pomegranates. Filled with olive oil and honey. A land without lack. The stones were iron and out of the hills they would dig copper. When they had eaten and were full, they would bless the LORD their God for the good land that He has given them. There was always the danger of the people forgetting the Lord by not keeping His commandments, His judgments, and His statutes.

How could that happen? Well, when you look further at Deut. 8:11-17, you see that the concern was that when they:

- Had more than enough food.

- Built beautiful houses and dwelt in them.

- Their herds and flocks were multiplied.

- Their silver and their gold were multiplied.

- All that they had were multiplied.

- Their hearts were lifted up.

They might say in their hearts that they had gained this wealth by their own hands, their own power, and their own might.

When the people of God became rich and full, they might deny God. Think about it, when things are going well with you, do you ask for help or rely on others? Same thing here, who would need God when they had everything? Who would need God when they could do all things by themselves? It is so easy to become relaxed and complacent when all things seem well. How quickly you forget that *"it is God who has made us and not we ourselves."* (Psa. 100:3) God knows every facet of your being and knew how to deal with this issue of self-sufficiency and self-boasting that plagued the children of Israel and which is so pervasive in mankind on a whole.

How does God deal with this issue? He leads you on a journey of trusting and obeying Him through "life trials." What you have to recognize is that each man's journey is unique to the purpose that God has for his life. You cannot afford to "rubberneck" and wonder "why is John or Sally not facing this, etc." Hello, their road is just that, their road; to bring them to their unique purpose in life.

Your attempt to travel someone else's "wilderness road" will not take you to your destiny. On the contrary, your attempt at using someone else's path for your own life will surely lead to sorrow, disappointment, and an aborted purpose.

The one size (one road) fits all does not work in this instance. Just as you have a distinct fingerprint, you also have a distinct purpose, a distinct plan from God the Father for your life.

Thus, trusting and obeying God is key. Where there is no faith, there can be no righteousness. The righteous shall live by faith in trusting and obeying Him. Your salvation does not begin and end with the acceptance of Christ as Lord. It is a complete journey from justification to glorification. *"And those He predestined, He also called; those He called, He also justified; those He justified, He also glorified."* Rom. 8:30 (NIV) Between justification and glorification is the sanctification (setting apart) process, the wilderness journey.

To leave Egypt was one thing but, to enter the Promised Land was a whole new ballgame altogether. Strategically located between the two was the wilderness. In essence, the impending wilderness experience becomes their sanctification process. The Passover was an external event that delivered Israel out of Egypt. But the wilderness experience served as the internal event to remove the stain of the Egyptian ways from their hearts and minds. It was to sanctify Israel. It was there God began to humble them and to test them to expose the intent of their hearts, whether they would keep His commandments or not.

It is no different today. You may not have to travel a considerable distance to experience your sanctifying event. But there are everyday challenges that present themselves and work to test the true fabric of your heart in the situation, whether or not you will trust God in the matter or lean to your own understanding. Prov. 3:5-6 reminds us to: *"Trust in the Lord with all thine heart; and lean not unto thine own understanding. In all thy ways acknowledge him, and he shall direct thy paths."*

The wilderness removes the crutches that tend to keep you from total dependence on God and forces you to be with God and no one else. When you actually take the time to allow the wilderness experiences to process you, you will begin to see Who God is and who you are as He reveals Himself to you.

One of the greatest obstacles in moving forward in the things of God is your human tendency to hold on to what is familiar, regardless of how painful and harmful the familiar may be. You also tend to resist change regardless of how promising it appears and the good it can bring.

It is the false security of the familiar that caused Israel to murmur against God in the wilderness. They wanted to go back to Egypt when they faced the unfamiliar in the desert. In Egypt,

IS THERE A DREAM? | 82

they knew at least what to expect. Although slaves, they had a routine and had become comfortable. They could count on things being provided even in the worst of conditions. But now in the wilderness, their dependency had to be on God to supply their needs.

It was in the wilderness experience that God revealed Himself to His people. He provided for them physically and He also gave them His laws and commandments. The commandments were the terms and conditions required for them to live freely and prosper in the Promised Land.

The Israelites spent more than four hundred years in Egypt. Throughout those years, they had become fully indoctrinated with the Egyptian ways and the Egyptian style of leadership, manners and customs. The Israelites did not realize that four hundred years of slavery also caused them to be trapped emotionally and spiritually.

They never experienced God in this manner and thus did not know Him nor His ways. Although delivered out of the hand of Pharaoh by mighty signs and wonders, the Israelites could not enjoy real freedom. Internally, they were still trapped in their own thoughts and understanding of how things should work. Their ways were not God's ways. To live in the Promised Land, the same way they lived in Egypt would have been detrimental to their existence.

They had been slaves; no doubt they would make slaves out of their own people, and become slave drivers themselves. When you think about it, that was the only way they knew. That was the method they saw working successfully in the so called land of pyramids and sphinx. They would have easily reverted to the familiar. There is a saying, *"you can take the pig out of the mud but, you can't take the mud out of the pig."* No matter how much you clean the pig up he will always go back to what he knows…wallowing in the mud.

God wanted to set them free completely so that they would be able to live well and prosper in the Promised Land. You have to realize that mental freedom is just as important as physical freedom.

Egypt remained in their hearts even after they had left. Think about it, four hundred years of bondage, seeing, being, and doing the same thing; Egypt was ingrained in them. The signs and wonders of God came and went, no longer thrilling them. Their first resort, when faced with hardship, was to go back to slavery when "their ways" did not work out in the wilderness. God had to discipline

them just as parents discipline their children.

However, Israel could neither understand nor

accept God's process of sanctification. Neither

could they grasp the love of God. The way God was

dealing with them was foreign and just like

everything else when you do not understand a

matter you tend to reject it. All Israel wanted was

the fulfillment of the promise of God and the

Promised Land. Wow! Doesn't that sound familiar?

How often does the believer press for the "blessings

of God" and not God himself?

In the wilderness, everything was the exact

opposite of the Promised Land, a land flowing with

milk and honey. All the promises of God from

beginning to fulfillment required faith and patience

(i.e. such as Noah building an ark, Abraham having

a son, and the manner in which the Messiah would come.) The main purpose of the wilderness was to prepare Israel's heart so that their faith could be built upon solid a foundation, God himself.

It was only in the wilderness that the Israelites could build a place for God so that He could dwell among them. The wilderness required their dependence on God for everything from bread to drink, to cloths, etc. The total dependence on God would lead them to an intimate and personal relationship with Him. Yet disobedience was the order of the day, they kept rejecting His laws and commands.

After moving in countless circles for forty long years, they remained untaught and unchanged. They basically got on God's last nerve so much so that He wanted to destroy them. In Exod. 33:3

(NLT), God said, *"But I will not travel among you, for you are a stubborn and rebellious people. If I did, I would surely destroy you along the way."* Though the Israelites faced some of their greatest difficulties in the wilderness, they also experienced some of their glorious encounters with God. Although, at the time, they could not see or understand that to be alone in the desert with God was a blessing and not a curse.

Sad to say spiritual slavery was not only evident in Israel; it is also evident in the Church today. How many times have you witnessed someone who says they have "known the Lord" for countless years? When you look at the evidence of their earthly existence (actions and attitudes), nothing of it denotes life much less a close relationship with God. In essence, they have remained untaught and unchanged. When you have a **genuine** encounter with God, change happens. It is just that simple because nothing outside of God can withstand the presence of God.

The journey of life's trials (wilderness experiences) will transform you into the pre-destined image God has for your life. If, and only if you purpose to develop your relationship with God, and you surrender your heart to obey and trust Him. It all begins with the heart position and your willingness to surrender your will to God so that the Excellency of Christ is formed in you.

CHAPTER SIX

Refocus - Let Go And Let God!

"Every day you spend drifting away from your goals is a waste not only of that day, but also of the additional day it takes to regain lost ground."

Ralph Martson

IF your significance as a person or your sense of security is tied to anything other than your relationship with God worry will choke the very life out of you.

"When you depend on another's perceptions to match your expectations you're setting yourself up for disappointment."

Tony Pearce

True happiness and peace lie in trusting God for what you need; knowing if it is right He will provide it and if it is not He will give you something better. Remember God sees the whole picture. You try to base your decisions on the little micro view you just happen to glimpse...what a waste.

There are so many nuggets such as wisdom, patience, understanding, etc. gleaned from the wilderness journey. Will it come overnight, no; will it be easy and palatable, definitely not. But, I can promise you that it will have been worthwhile.

Just allow the Holy Spirit to mold and shape you into the image that God has already predestined you to become. He alone knows how the blueprint for your life looks. He will only follow the instructions received from God. According to John 16:13, *"Howbeit when he the Spirit of truth, is come, he will guide you into all truth: for he shall not speak of himself; but whatsoever he shall hear, that shall he speak: and he will shew you things to come."*

If you are not sure about what you should do, wait; if you do not understand a matter, listen. The Holy Spirit is right there with the right instruction for the right time; you only have to trust Him in the process.

As stated before, there will be numerous wilderness journeys as each one is designed to address a particular issue in your life. Your journey will not be like mine, and neither will my journey be like yours. Just as each person has a distinct fingerprint so are the wilderness experiences of each life. They are expressly designed to leave an indelible imprint on your heart.

All too often you dismiss dreams as something that you went to bed thinking about or maybe they were the result of some food you ate. I mean really, food? Neither are they some idea you conjured up in your mind. All dreams have a source and a purpose. However, you have to be discerning as to whether or not that source is divine or intellectual. Know this, things do not just happen. Everything in God is purposeful. And even in the worst of circumstances you have the comfort in knowing that according to Romans 8:28 *"... we know that all things work together for good to them that love God, to them who are called according to his purpose."*

Your dream will never come to fruition without you having completed the lessons of the wilderness experience. It is those distinct experiences that will strengthen, encourage, establish and propel you into your future. Allowing the Holy Spirit to speak to your heart and to direct your path is critical to maximizing the experience of the wilderness journey. Do not let the familiarity of a situation force you to take matters into your own hands by making decisions without the benefit of the counsel of the Holy Spirit. If you do so, you will find that you have ended up wasting a lot of precious time. In the end, you will have to go back to the beginning.

Also, you will have the honor (sic) of walking out the mess you created when you ventured off on your own in the first place. Yep, I am speaking from personal experience. After a few bumps on "wilderness road," I learned quickly to check my thoughts and actions against the Word of God and the Holy Spirit. If they did not line up, then I had to learn to let it go or leave it alone. Otherwise, I would only be headed for hardship and heartache both of which I can do without, and I am sure you would agree.

Granted, knowing what to do in every situation and circumstance is difficult, especially if you are trying to handle things on your own. In this wilderness journey, you have to acknowledge to yourself that you do not know everything. It is that simple. Why stress yourself out? The Holy Spirit stands by patiently waiting to lead you and guide you, but your pride says otherwise, "I got this; I know what to do." Just stop. Surrender your will daily to the Lord and watch Him work everything out. I learned long ago to say "I do not know, but I know Who does!" It works every time. You only miss the mark when you go off in your own strength, doing things your own way.

Self-sufficiency is an effective tool used by Satan to entrap and stifle the usefulness of the body of Christ. You must learn to rest and enjoy the solace of the Wilderness Road that God has called you to take. Keeping in mind that if God has called you to it, He has already provided the grace for it. Just walk it out.

In this hour, it is important that you learn to prioritize your time and your talents. Do not get so busy doing things that you miss God. It is so easy to get caught up doing things for God, and in the name of God that God has not required you to do. It is Satan's role to keep you busy and get you sidetracked from your true purpose. Retrain your ear to hear the voice of the Lord. Know that relationships are important. That was established in the beginning when God created Adam and communed with him in the garden. He has always desired a relationship with His creation.

And thus, with His creation called "mankind" having been made in His image, the desire should be in you to have a relationship with Him and value your relationship with others also. God came in the form of Christ reconciling the world back to Himself because He desires a relationship with His people, not things.

CHAPTER SEVEN

Is There A Dream?

By now you are probably saying, "okay about all this wilderness stuff but what about my dream?"

What about your dream? First, you need to determine if your dream is real or fantasy? Is this really what God has for you or is it just something you wish would happen? How many times have you asked those questions of yourself?

What is the difference between a God-given dream and an illusion? For one, if the dream is truly from God, you have the innate ability and calling to achieve it. According to Merriam-Webster's dictionary an *illusion* is *"a state of being intellectually deceived;"* what I like to call "living in your head" and one in which you will not have the ability or grace to achieve.

How do you know if your dream will come true or what should you do once you've determined that it is from God? Essentially, there are seven key elements for your dream to come true.

First, write it down. *"Write the vision, and make it plain upon the tables, that he may run that readeth it."* (Hab. 2:2) Do not depend on your memory because as soon as another thought enters your mind you will find yourself trying to remember the dream. Be realistic. If you were about to take a trip to a new place you would naturally write down all the information on how to get there. Or in this day and age, input the coordinates in the GPS and follow the instructions succinctly. Well, your dream is part of the roadmap to your future. If you want to get to your future, write it down. You cannot efficiently arrive at a destination without envisioning where you are going. You must have something to follow. You have to know where you are going, and you cannot be afraid to try or fail.

Second, God-given dreams require great patience. *"For the vision is yet for an appointed time, but at the end it shall speak, and not lie: though it tarry, wait for it; because it will surely come, it will not tarry."* (Hab. 2:3) Remember, Joseph's dream took almost thirteen years to come to pass and let us not forget about Moses' forty years. So, just chillax.

Third, God-given dreams are often born from pain. History books state that Abraham Lincoln stood on the dock of a New Orleans shipyard and saw a screaming child torn from his mother's arms and sold away into slavery. Having witnessed this, he dug his fingernails into his hands until they were bleeding. Because of this scene, he dreamed of a day when America would be free of the curse of slavery. His dream helped him through a nervous breakdown and ten political defeats before he eventually became president of the United States. After much political wrangling, he signed the Emancipation Proclamation and his dream came true. Do not stop until you have what God has for you.

Fourth, God-given dreams come from God, not other people. Many times people are lured into a situation because someone told them, "I see you doing this" or "I think you would be better at that." Whatever the person is saying to you, if it is from God it will bear witness with your spirit and only confirm what you already know to be true in your heart by the Spirit of God. You must learn to hear the voice of God for yourself.

Fifth, God-given dreams are sustained by favor from God. Although a servant in Potiphar's house, Joseph found favor with his master; and though unjustly imprisoned he found favor with the jailer and eventually favor with Pharaoh. There is a phrase in the Bible that follows Joseph all the way through his story, "The Lord was with him." When the Lord is with you, without a doubt, the favor will come.

Sixth, uncommon dreams require unusual preparation. Joseph prepared for thirteen years; Moses spent eighty years getting ready for a forty-year ministry. Additionally, Jesus prepared thirty years for a ministry of three and a half years. How long is long enough? Good question.

Lastly, God-given dreams will create enemies. Joseph's brothers, because of jealousy, threw him into the pit, and Potiphar's wife had him thrown into prison. Thus, if you are living without opposition, you are likely living an illusion. If you have no resistance, you are not doing anything worthwhile. Please note, if it were easy, everybody would be doing it. The wilderness experience serves as the preparation for God-given dream fulfillment that is directly related to your purpose and destiny. The innate abilities you have within you must be cultivated, enhanced, sharpened, and nurtured to ensure your success when the pivotal moment arrives in your life.

I encourage you to accept this invitation with gladness recognizing that your *"light affliction is but for a moment" (2 Cor 4.17).* How long is a moment? God can answer that one for you when you meet Him in the wilderness.

EPILOGUE

You are living in a time of unprecedented
uncertainty. What you thought you knew you did
not; and what you thought was, is not anymore. As
you look around you find that no one really knows
where to go, what to do or who to turn to. It is what
I would call the "Great Setup." Because until now,
every man has proceeded to do what was right in
his own eyes failing to realize that their outcome
was destined for destruction.

Today, you see each country across the globe struggling to find an answer; strategizing to get a grip on this tidal wave of economic destruction, political unrest, and religious friction. All the great minds in academia, business, politics, and religion have pulled from their luscious bags of tricks. Each trying to devise a pathway out of this quagmire of economic, political, and religious chaos, yet they have been and will continue to be unsuccessful.

In each one's earnestness to be "the one" to discover "the answer" neither has come to realize that in their frame called humanity, they are limited in their understanding. Where they should be searching they dare not; whom they should be asking, they ask not. Why? Because their minds are settled in darkness, and the light of revelation will never come to those who choose the path of self-reliance.

Hence, there has now come the clarion call from the Spirit of the living God to those that have an ear to hear. As each day passes the call grows stronger and stronger like waves of the ocean coming ashore. It is the sound of heaven. A call to the remnant of God to rise in their spheres of influence and command the Kingdom to come and God's will to be done in the face of adversity and uncertainty.

This sound is of a frequency only heard by those who are willing to shed the skin of earth's trappings, those things that would easily sidetrack and distract from the work at hand. Their sole purpose is to do and say only that which the Father has commanded. They are not moved by the political will, personal gain or self-promotion. They are a people who have counted the cost and are willing and committed to going the distance regardless of the challenges of the time. They are not moved by rejection, ridicule, public sentiment or angst. Their call is clear, their focus is sure and their commitment is unwavering. They are the Called Out! The First Fruit of this new move of God.

Can you hear the sound? It is time to release The Sound of Heaven in the marketplace.

REFLECTIONS

"What Next?

I hope that after reading this book you will take the time to reflect on your own life and see where you may have hindered the will of God by escaping the wilderness experiences that were necessary for your life's plan. You can start by asking yourself the follow questions:

1. What is my dream?

2. Is it God-given or is it an illusion?

3. What is required for me to achieve it?

4. Am I willing to relinquish control of my life to God and surrender to the process "sight unseen" by allowing the Holy Spirit to direct my steps?

5. What is God requiring me to do today that I have not yielded to doing?

6. Am I in the wilderness now? If so, do I understand why?

7. How much do I really trust and believe that God can and will do for me what He has done for others?

8. Do I really want all that God has for me and am I willing to pay the price to attain it?

The wilderness journey will consists of a lifetime of experiences. Don't shortchange your future by trying to escape them. Each journey is **essential** for you to arrive at your future.

NOTES

Forward
1. "Wilderness." *Merriam-Webster*. Merriam-Webster. Web. 17 July. 2015.

Chapter 1
1. "Status Quo." *Merriam-Webster*. Merriam-Webster. Web. 3 Jan. 2015.
2. "Norm." *Merriam-Webster*. Merriam-Webster. Web. 3 Jan. 2015.
3. Mandela, Nelson. "Nelson Mandela Quotes." *BrainyQuote*. Xplore. Web. 14 Jan. 2015.
4. Amplified Bible. Bible Gateway. Web. 15 Jan. 2015
5. Matthews, Marisa D. "Conversation." Personal interview. 2 Feb. 2015.
6. Ibid.
7. Clark, Frank A. "Frank A. Clark Quotes." BrainyQuote. Xplore. Web. 16 Feb. 2015.
8. Tozer, A.W. "The Gaze of the Soul." *The Pursuit of God*. [31 January 2011] ed. Christian Miracle Foundation, 2011. Print.
9. Marston, Ralph. "Ralph Marston Quotes." *BrainyQuote*. Xplore. Web. 9 Jan. 2015.
10. Peale, Norman Vincent. "Norman Vincent Peale Quote." *BrainyQuote*. Xplore. Web. 2 Mar. 2015.

Chapter 2
1. Maxwell, John. "John C. Maxwell Quote." *BrainyQuote*. Xplore. Web. 28 Mar. 2015.
2. Rohn, Jim. "Jim Rohn Quote." *Goodreads*. Web. 6 Apr. 2015.

Chapter 3

1. Matthews, Marisa D. "Conversation." Personal interview. 21 Apr. 2015.
2. Peterson, Eugene H. *The Message: The Bible in Contemporary Language*. Colorado Springs: NavPress, 2002. Print.
3. Maxwell, John. "John C. Maxwell Quote." *BrainyQuote*. Xplore. Web. 10 May 2015.

Chapter 4

1. Author Unknown
2. Isaac, Brad. "Abe Lincoln's Productivity Secret." *Persistence Unlimited*. 29 Jan. 2006. Web. 26 June 2015.
3. *The Ten Commandments*. Perf. Charlton Heston, Yul Brynner. Parmount Pictures, 1956. Film.
4. *The Prince of Egypt*. Perf. Val Kilmer, Ralph Fiennes, Sandra Bullock, Michelle Pfeiffer. DreamWorks, 1998. Film.
5. "Syndrome." *Merriam-Webster*. Merriam-Webster. Web. 28 Jul.2015

Chapter 5

1. Ong, Joshua. "Entering The Promised Land." *The Josh Link*. Web. 17 Feb. 2015.
2. *New International Version*. Bible Gateway. Web. 17 Feb. 2015
3. *New Living Translation*. Bible Gateway. Web. 18 Feb. 2015

Chapter 6

1. Cottrell, David. "The Second Monday: Keep the Main Thing the Main Thing." *Monday Morning Leadership: 8 Mentoring Sessions You Can't Afford to Miss*. Dallas: CornerStone Leadership Institute, 2002. 29. Print.
2. Marston, Ralph. "Ralph Marston Quote." *BrainyQuote*. Xplore. Web. 6 May 2015.

Chapter 7

1. Mack, Jay. "Genesis Commentary." *The Teaching Ministry of Jay Mack - Where Life and the Bible Meet*. Web. 15 June 2015.
2. "Illusion." *Merriam-Webster*. Merriam-Webster. 28 Jul. 2015.
3. William H. Herndon and Jesse W. Weik, *Herndon's Life of Abraham Lincoln*.

ACKNOWLEDGMENTS

It is said that the journey of a thousand miles begins with the first step. Though I have been walking all my life, I view my first step being the time I truly committed my heart and mind to the Lord Jesus Christ. It was not until then that I could have an inkling of what God had in store for my life. I Cor 2:9: *"But as it is written, EYE HATH NOT SEE, NOR EAR HEARD, NEITHER HAVE ENTERED INTO THE HEART OF MAN, THE THINGS WHICH GOD HATH PREPARED FOR THEM THAT LOVE HIM."*

I am thankful to God for the people He has placed in my life over the years to nurture me in "all things Christ." Pastor Claudette M. Basden who is my spiritual mom, mentor, and best friend. I thank God that you allowed the Holy Spirit to use you to preach a message in 2002 that awakened purpose in my life.

Thanks Pastor Laurice A. Brown for your unconditional love and encouragement.

Thanks to Millicent Grant for enduring countless questions while I waited not so patiently for you to review my initial draft. You keep it real.

Thanks to my baby sister Joi James, who has always encouraged me to follow my passion and has laughingly over the years dubbed me the "Dale Carnegie" of the family.

Thanks, Dad (Matt), for your loving way of instilling confidence without saying a single word.

You let me know that the only thing that could ever stop me would be me and to never let that happen.

And it goes without saying that Mom (Apostle Dorothy L. Matthews) was key in laying the foundation in my life that "without God, I can do nothing." It was from that position that Matt. 6:33 became the cornerstone of my walk with God. *"But seek ye first the kingdom of God, and his righteousness; and all these things shall be added unto you."*

To the rest of my friends and family, it would take another book to name you all. Thanks for your love and support and I pray whatever good you see in me you will give God the glory because it is because of Him that I am who I am today.

ABOUT THE AUTHOR

MARISA D. MATTHEWS was born in San Francisco, California, the second child of retired Naval Chief William A. Matthews and Apostle Dorothy Matthews. Her father's Navy career enabled her to travel internationally at a young age and become introduced to various customs and ways of life.

She holds a Bachelor's degree in Accounting with a minor in Business Information Systems, an Executive Master's degree in Business Administration with international finance emphasis, and an Executive Juris Doctor. With over thirty years of diverse experience in the financial, manufacturing, retail and non-profit sectors she has held key management positions with Fortune 500 companies.

An expert in her field, she is called to speak on topics ranging from business reorganization, change management, financial empowerment, leadership development and Kingdom leadership in the marketplace to name a few. Her wealth of knowledge and expertise in management and leadership has carried her extensively throughout North America and the Caribbean and has been recognized globally.

She is the CEO of Dominion International Consulting, a firm devoted to assisting individuals and businesses in identifying untapped resources to create opportunities for growth and advancement in their respective spheres of influence yielding positive bottom-line results.

Equally fulfilling is her passion for youth and ministry where she continues to provide leadership, financial, academic and professional development for youth and a host of business professionals since 1991.

She is an ordained minister of A Touch of Love Ministries International Center, Inc. – Providenciales, Turks and Caicos Islands and the Academic Advisor and adjunct instructor for Champions for Christ International School of Excellence – Providenciales, Turks and Caicos Islands; along with a host of other board affiliations.

She is a Certified Public Accountant, Certified Global Management Accountant, and a Certified Information Technology Professional. Her desire is to share and impart her professional knowledge and experience into the development of "Kingdom-minded" marketplace leaders for the next generation.

She is proud and blessed to have in her life son-in-law Kendrick, daughter Maria, son Javaughn, and granddaughter, Gabrielle.